Nature and Grace

in Herman Bavinck

NATURE AND GRACE

IN

HERMAN BAVINCK

Jan Veenhof

Translated by Albert M. Wolters

Dordt College Press

The main text in this booklet was translated from the Dutch by Albert M. Wolters from J. Veenhof, *Revelatie en Inspiratie* (Amsterdam: Buijten en Schipperheijn, 1968), 345–365.

Dordt College Press   www.dordt.edu/dordt_press
498 Fourth Avenue NE
Sioux Center, Iowa 51250
United States of America

ISBN-13: 978-0-932914-69-9
ISBN-10: 0-932914-69-1

Library of Congress Cataloging-in-Publication Data

Veenhof, Jan, 1934-
   [Revelatie en inspiratie. English]
   Nature and grace in Herman Bavinck / Jan Veenhof ; translated by Albert M. Wolters.
      p. cm.
   Includes bibliographical references.
   ISBN-13: 978-0-932914-69-9 (pbk. : alk. paper)
   1. Bavinck, Herman, 1854-1921. 2. Theology, Doctrinal--History
--19th century.   I. Title.
BX9479.B35V413 2006
230'.42092--dc22
                                        2006026896

Cover design: Rob Haan

Table of Contents

Translator's Preface

Herman Bavinck (1854–1921) was a noted Reformed theologian, chiefly known for his four-volume *Gereformeerde Dogmatiek* (second edition, 1906–1911). He is one of the two giants (next to Abraham Kuyper) of the great revival of Calvinism (sometimes called Neocalvinism) in nineteenth-century Holland. In his later years he also published extensively in the fields of philosophy, psychology, and educational theory, and he was active in politics.

The booklet is a translation of twenty pages from Jan Veenhof's dissertation on Bavinck, entitled *Revelatie en Inspiratie* (Amsterdam: Buijten en Schipperheijn, 1968). Veenhof was the successor of G.C. Berkouwer in the chair for dogmatic theology at the Free University in Amsterdam. His dissertation is a massive, 700-page work that treats Bavinck's doctrine of revelation in the context both of Bavinck's thought as a whole and of the competing theological currents of his day, especially the so-called "ethical" movement.

Within this much broader scope, the pages on nature and grace are only a small sub-section. Nevertheless, they are of pivotal importance, since they deal with what has been called "the central theme of Bavinck's thought." They bring together, in short compass, Bavinck's major statements on this theme, and they are put in context by a scholar who can lay claim to being one of today's leading authorities on Bavinck.

However, these pages are of interest not just for students of Bavinck's theology: Bavinck's statement of the basic thesis that grace restores nature, or that salvation means the restoration of creation, is of far wider significance. It puts in a succinct formulation a dimension of biblical teaching that has been the distinctive strength of the Calvinist tradition of Christian thought, both in theology and in a wide range of other academic disciplines.

Bavinck's thought in general and his emphasis on creation in particular (understood broadly in terms of creation ordinances for all of life and reality) are also of great significance for understanding the so-called Amsterdam school of philosophy, which builds directly on Bavinck's insights in this regard. D. H. T. Vollenhoven, one of the two founders of this philosophical school, became a student of Bavinck's at the Free University in 1911, the year when Bavinck published his last theological book. For the remaining decade of his life, Bavinck turned almost exclusively to the application of Calvinist principles to other disciplines. During seven of these years, Vollenhoven was Bavinck's student and disciple, first in theology, then in philosophy. In 1918 Vollenhoven received his doctorate with a dissertation on the philosophy of mathematics from a theistic point of view; he then began his life's work of elaborating a Calvinistic philosophy. After some years, he was joined in this work by his wife's brother, Herman Dooyeweerd, a brilliant young legal theorist of Calvinist persuasion who had discovered the importance of philosophical questions for the theoretical foundations of law. During the decade of the 1920s, the two elaborated together the basic outline of their common philosophy, widely known as the "philosophy of the cosmonomic idea," a name directly linked to the Calvinist emphasis on creation ordinances.

Central to the religious vision underlying the cosmonomic philosophy is Bavinck's insight that grace restores nature, i.e., that creation is not abolished but integrally renewed by salvation in Christ. In Vollenhoven, this insight comes out in many typically Bavinckian formulations in his writings and in his treatment of the good-evil distinction as a primary dimension irreducible to any creational distinctions. In Dooyeweerd the impact of Bavinck's fundamental thesis can be discerned in his formulation of the Christian "ground-motive" (Creation, Fall, Redemption) and in his analysis of the nature-grace ground-motive in Roman Catholicism and elsewhere.

This is not to say that Vollenhoven and Dooyeweerd have not substantially altered the *formulation* of Bavinck's insight. Bavinck's conceptual apparatus is borrowed very largely from Neothomism, whereas Vollenhoven and Dooyeweerd have evolved a categorial framework and terminology of their own, which do fuller justice to the religious intuition of Calvinism. This framework and terminology are particularly evident in their use of the categories "law," "subject," and "direction," which replace Bavinck's Neothomist categories "substance" and "accidents," to express the effects of sin in creation. Where Bavinck speaks of sin as "accidental" to the "substance" of creation, Vollenhoven and Dooyeweerd speak of a change in religious "direction" within the subject-side of creation, leaving the law-side (or "structure") unaffected by sin.

Bavinck's central intuition that grace restores nature is therefore pivotal for an understanding of both the distinctive genius of Calvinism and the vigorous philosophical movement to which it has given birth. It is, moreover, of great relevance to the renewed discussion of the doctrine of creation in contemporary theology. Veenhof's summary of his position is, therefore, an invaluable resource.

A few words should be said about the translation (revised 1980). Veenhof's Dutch text has been closely followed, with only editorial alterations. These include the italicization of foreign words, the attempt to bring out biblical allusions by using the language of the King James Version (just as Bavinck's usage reflects the language of the *Statenvertaling*), the insertion of headings and block quotations to break up the text, and the expansion of Veenhof's bibliographical abbreviations in the notes. There is an exception on the last point for references to Bavinck's four-volume *Gereformeerde Dogmatiek* (Kampen, vierde druk, 1928–30), which are simply cited in the form "I 325," "III 85," etc. Furthermore, page references to English translations of Bavinck's works have been added where applicable, although quoted passages were, in each case, freshly translated. Cross-references and allusions to other parts of Veenhof's text have been left unchanged.

The following renderings of individual words deserve note. *Wetenschap* is usually translated "scholarship," sometimes "science." *Maatschappij* is translated "society," although this term is potentially misleading, since it strictly refers to "civil society" (*bürgerliche Gesellschaft*), thus excluding family, state and church. However, the context generally prevents misunderstanding. It is difficult to render in English the distinction Bavinck makes between *restauratie* and *herstel* (p. 25), since both of these would normally be translated "restoration" in other contexts. I have chosen to reserve "restoration" for *herstel* (because of its greater frequency and to conform with English theological usage), and to use "repristination" for *restauratie*. The reader should keep in mind (though my rendering now obscures the fact) that the latter word carried strong overtones of the historically reactionary movements of the nineteenth century and that Bavinck is consciously exploiting this pejorative connotation.

It remains for me to thank professor Veenhof for his kindness in allowing this use of his dissertation material. This I do gladly and with full sincerity. For scores of English-speaking students, this short paper has already been a clear window to the distinctive strengths of Dutch Neocalvinism. For others it has become a door. For my own part, the translation has been a labor of love.

Addendum (2006). The above was written in 1980 and served as preface to the last revision of this translation, which was originally done in 1977. It was for many years available (in mimeographed form) from the Institute for Christian Studies in Toronto, and I am delighted that it is now, after twenty-six years, appearing in print. In the intervening years English translations of four of Bavinck's publications have appeared in English, and I have taken the opportunity of incorporating references to them in this printed version of Veenhof's essay. The translations in question are the following: (1) *De zekerheid des geloofs,* translated by Harry der Nederlanden as *The Certainty of Faith* (St. Catharines, ON: Paideia Press, 1980); (2) *De algemeene genade* (1888), translated by Raymond C. Van Leeuwen as "Common Grace," *Calvin Theological Journal* 24 (1989) 35–65; (3) *De katholiciteit van christendom en kerk* (1888), translated by John Bolt as "The Catholicity of Christianity and the Church," *Calvin Theological Journal* 27 (1992) 220–51; (4) the first three volumes of Bavinck's *magnum opus, Gereformeerde Dogmatiek* (second edition, 1906–1911), translated by John Vriend under the editorship of John Bolt as *Reformed Dogmatics* (Grand Rapids: Baker Academic, 2003–2006). Where these works are quoted in the following, I have not revised my translation to conform to them, but in the footnotes I have now added, in brackets, the appropriate page numbers of these new English translations. Thus in *"De algemeene genade,* p. 21 [ET 48]," the bracketed number gives the page number in Van Leeuwen's English translation (ET) that corresponds to p. 21 in the Dutch. References to the *Gereformeerde Dogmatiek* are given in the form "I 330 [ET 1.360]." Unfortunately, volume 4 of the *Reformed Dogmatics* has not yet appeared in English, although its concluding section on eschatology was published separately as *The Last Things: Hope for this World and the Next* (1996). Since this section is to be incorporated (with different pagination) in the forthcoming fourth volume, I have refrained altogether from giving translation page references for volume 4.

A. M. Wolters

Nature and Grace in Herman Bavinck

Introduction

Bavinck's view of the relation of nature and grace is a central part—indeed, perhaps we may even say *the* central theme—of his theology.[1] We have already come across this theme a number of times in the above. We propose now to pay special attention to it, at least insofar as this theme is necessary to illumine the structure of Bavinck's doctrine of revelation.

Because the essence of the Christian religion consists in the re-creation of the cosmos into a kingdom of God, Bavinck writes that "the great question, which returns always and everywhere," is this:

> how is grace related to nature . . . what is the connection between creation and re-creation, of the rich of the earth and the kingdom of heaven, of humanity and Christianity, of that which is below and that which is above?[2]

It is the ancient question as to what relationship must be established between the Gospel of Christ and culture in the broadest sense of the word. This question presents itself in all kinds of forms, but it is always the same problem that is at issue, a problem which is a matter of concern, not just to a single period but in every age, and which

> definitely does not exist only for theoretical thinking, but urges itself upon every person in the practical affairs of life. All movements and schools that lay claim to the lives and minds of men can be described and judged according to the position that they take on *this* question of principle.[3]

The fact is that Bavinck reduces all divergences among Christians to differences concerning this fundamental problem:

> Every Christian must take into account two factors: creation and re-creation, nature and grace, earthly and heavenly vocation, etc.; and in accordance with the different relationship in which he puts these to each other, his religious life assumes a different character. Man's relationship to God is determinative of his relationship to things in general. Whoever breaks the divinely appointed connection between nature and grace is led to sacrifice one to the other. Socinianism and Anabaptism, Rationalism and Mysticism are the resulting deviant paths into which the Christian goes astray.[4]

This fundamental problem engaged Bavinck's interest from the very beginning. His first somewhat extended statement on the problematics involved is to be found in his essay on the theology of Ritschl. The passage concerned is especially significant because it sheds a revealing light on Bavinck's own questions and uncertainties. For the sake of clarity, we quote it in full:

> Therefore, whereas salvation in Christ was formerly considered primarily a means to separate man from sin and the world, to prepare him for heavenly blessedness and to cause him to enjoy undisturbed fellowship with God there, Ritschl posits the very opposite relationship: the purpose of salvation in Christ is precisely to enable a person, once he is freed from the oppressive feeling of sin and lives in the awareness of being a child of God, to exercise his earthly vocation and fulfill his moral purpose in this world. The antithesis, therefore, is fairly sharp: on the one side a Christian life that considers the highest goal, now and hereafter, to be the contemplation of God and fellowship with him, and for that reason (always being more or less hostile to the riches of an earthly life) is in danger of falling into monasticism and asceticism, pietism and mysticism; but on the side of Ritschl, a Christian life that considers its highest goal to be the kingdom of God, i.e., the moral obligation of mankind, and for that reason (always being more or less averse to the withdrawal into solitude and quiet communion with God), is in danger of degenerating into a cold Pelagianism and an unfeeling moralism.

Personally, I do not yet see any way of combining the two points of view, but I do know that there is much that is excellent in both, and that both contain undeniable truth.[5]

Since Bavinck himself gives expression to his uncertainty, it is all the more of interest to examine Bavinck's later discussions of this theme. It was still in the same year in which the essay on Ritschl was published, 1888, that Bavinck delivered his rectorial oration on the catholicity of Christianity and the church, in which he dealt extensively with the nature-grace relation. This was supplemented and further elaborated in the 1894 rectorial oration on common grace. These two publications from Bavinck's first period provide us with his most extensive treatment of the subject under discussion and also undoubtedly constitute the best source for getting to know Bavinck's thoughts on the matter. All the subsequent discussions in Bavinck's writings about the relation of nature and grace (and they are considerable) can be considered a further explication and undergirding of his argument in these two orations. Accordingly, it is in the first place from these two speeches that we have chiefly drawn our materials for this section; in the notes (and later on also in the text) we have identified and quoted passages from other publications as well.

Confrontation with Roman Catholicism

As always, Bavinck develops his own viewpoint in constant critical confrontation with all kinds of schools of thought, past and present, in this case primarily with Roman Catholicism.[6] It is really impossible to disengage Bavinck's own views on nature and grace from his dignified but incisive polemics. We will do well, therefore, not to leave aside this critique but to include it in our analysis.

Bavinck reminds us that the concept "world" is used in two

senses in the New Testament. Firstly, it denotes the world insofar as the world is fallen under the dominion of sin, but secondly, it also denotes that same world insofar as the world has been the object of God's love. In this connection he refers, among other texts, to John 3:16 and 17—passages that play an important role in his discussions of nature and grace.[7] After the New Testament period, however, people soon began to deviate from this view of the world: "The two lines that are indicated by Scripture for our view of the world are not maintained and worked out equally."[8] In general, the early Christians had a strictly negative attitude toward the world and its culture: "The second and third centuries are full of dualism and asceticism." The church itself, witness her rejection of Montanism and Donatism, etc., did not want to take the road of asceticism and separatism. She wanted to be a world church and was successful in this, but not without having recognized and assimilated asceticism and monasticism as a legitimate element within her boundaries, although she continued to uphold the legitimacy of the lower ideal as well:[9] "In this way, the qualitative opposition that had originally existed between the world and the church was transformed into a quantitative one."[10]

It is at this point that the *principle* of the Roman Catholic worldview comes to the fore:

> In Roman Catholicism, "the world" more and more loses the ethical significance that it has in the Scriptures. That which is natural is not sinful, but it is that which constitutionally does not attain the supernatural. The supernatural is a *donum superadditum*. . . . Consequently Christianity and grace, which have entered the world to enable us to attain the supernatural, the *visio Dei*, do not reform and recreate the existing order, but only complement creation. Christianity transcendently supervenes upon the natural, but does not penetrate and sanctify it. Thereby Roman Catholicism, which calls itself catholic in a preeminent sense, has altered the nature of the catholicity of the New Testament. The catholicity of the Christian principle,

which purifies and sanctifies everything, has been replaced by the dualism that puts the supernatural in a separate position alongside, or rather in a transcendent position above the natural. Creation and re-creation remain two independent quantities over against each other.[11]

Catholicism, therefore, holds to a "juxtaposition of the natural and the supernatural order."[12] As a result, "The supernatural is an order of its own, aloof from the natural life, and sealed off from it on all sides."[13] In all this "the genius of the Roman Catholic system" is the principle of hierarchy. This principle explains the relatively favorable evaluation of the natural, which in Catholic thought is good in itself; it is only incomplete and needs complementation.[14] The root of the whole system, in Bavinck's judgment, is to be found in Pelagianism:

> If for a moment you abstract from the supernatural order that Catholicism has built up around the natural order, then you will have nothing left but pure rationalism, genuine Pelagianism, and unadulterated deism.[15]

The essence of the Catholic worldview is, therefore, that the natural is good in itself but belongs to a lower order:

> Catholicism, therefore, does indeed hold to the catholicity of Christianity insofar as Catholicism lays claim to the whole world and seeks to subordinate all things to the church. But this catholicity is denied in the sense that Christianity itself must permeate everything like a leaven. It remains an eternal dualism; Christianity does not become an immanent and reforming principle. This dualism is not an antinomy, in which one pole excludes the other. Catholicism does not annihilate the natural, in the manner of the Manichaeans, but devalues it. To be sure, it allows marriage, family, earthly vocation, the state, science and art to exist, and even gives to all of these, within the limits of their proper spheres, a much greater freedom to move than Protestantism does; but it depreciates and depresses the natural; it puts on everything the stamp of contempt and brands it as the profane. In Catholicism, the fundamental opposition is not that of holy and unholy, but of consecrated and profane. It reduces the ethical to the material, and looks upon the natural as

something non-divine not because and insofar as it is impure, but because it is incapable of attaining the supernatural. Catholicism makes the cosmos profane.[16]

⌈Hence, anything that passes from the domain of nature to that of the supernatural order must be consecrated.[17]⌋

With "this imposing Roman Catholic system the Reformation came into collision at virtually every point." The sixteenth-century Reformation was not only a reformation of the church but also an "entirely different and new conception of Christianity itself": The Reformers, going back to the New Testament, replaced the dualistic world and life view of Catholicism, and its quantitative opposition between the natural and the supernatural, "with a truly theistic worldview and a qualitative opposition."[18] The Reformation, "as begun by Luther and Zwingli, and reinforced and carried through by Calvin, put an end to the Romish supernaturalism and dualism and asceticism."[19] Because of the way in which the Reformation established the relation of nature and grace, the cosmos of course immediately gains significantly in importance. It "continues to be the primary, the original, the natural state, to which the Christian religion, the *foedus gratiae*, is intended to lead back":[20]

> The Reformation gave us a clearer understanding not only of the articles of faith concerning the Father and the Holy Spirit, concerning the church and forgiveness; it also rehabilitated the first article of our ecumenical Christian faith, and gave full weight to the confession: "I believe in God, the Father, Almighty, Creator of heaven and earth." In this, they rediscovered the natural, restored it to its rightful place, and freed it from the Roman Catholic stigma of being profane and unconsecrated. The natural is not something of lesser value and of a lower order, as though it were not susceptible to sanctification and renewal, but rather required only to be bridled and repressed. It is just as divine as the church, though it owes its origin not to re-creation but creation, though it is not from the Son but from the Father.[21]

In this way, the mechanical relation of nature and grace is replaced in Protestantism by an ethical one:

> [Christianity is not a quantitative entity that hovers transcendently above the natural, but a religious and ethical power that enters immanently within the natural and banishes only that which is impure. The kingdom of heaven may be a treasure and a pearl; it is also a mustard seed and a leaven.[22]]

This principial divergence between Roman Catholicism and the Reformation comes into sharp focus in the contrast with respect to the concept of grace. In Catholicism, writes Bavinck, grace has a double task: *ut elevet et sanet.* But the first completely overshadows the second. Grace is [necessary absolutely] in the first sense, but only [*per accidens*] in the second:

> Grace, in Catholicism, is in the first place a quality that is added to man above and beyond the natural order, and through which he is in principle taken up into a supernatural order, becomes a participant in the divine nature and the vision of God, and is enabled to accomplish the kind of supernatural works that *ex condigno* earn eternal life.[23]

The Reformation, however, rejected the Neoplatonic mysticism underlying this conception, of which the most important thing is the elevation of man above his nature, his deification; it

> returned to the simplicity of Holy Scripture, and therefore acquired an entirely different conception of grace. Grace does not serve to take man up into a supernatural order, but to liberate him from sin. [Grace is not opposed to nature, but only to sin.] Properly speaking, it was not necessary for Adam before the Fall, but has become necessary only because of sin; therefore, it is not necessary absolutely, but only *per accidens.* The physical opposition of natural and supernatural is replaced by the ethical one of sin and grace.

The function of grace is exclusively the removal of sin; if this happens, then man is automatically image of God again, for the image of God is not a *donum superadditum* but belongs to the essence of man. "There is thus no need for there to be, next to the grace that delivers from sin, another grace that moreover elevates man above his nature."[24]

A corollary of this is that grace in Reformation theology in no way can have the character of a substance. For that matter, the mere fact that sin is not a substance, and has not deprived man of anything substantial, means that grace can never be conceived of as a substance:

> It is a restoration of the *forma* that was impressed upon man and creatures in general at creation. Re-creation is not a second, new creation. It does not add any new creatures to the existing order, or introduce a new substance, but it is essentially reformation. In this, the operation of grace extends intensively as far as the power of sin. Sin has affected everything; it has corrupted the whole organism of creation, the very nature of creatures; and therefore grace is a power of God that liberates mankind from sin also inwardly, in the core of its being, and shall one day present it without spot or wrinkle before God's face.[25]

Confrontation with Other Protestant Traditions

The change that was effected by the Reformation in the Roman Catholic worldview was indeed nothing less than a complete revolution. In Bavinck's view, however, there did not exist a complete harmony among the Reformers. While Luther and Zwingli, each in his own way, were still caught in dualism to a certain extent, it remained for Calvin to overcome this dualism. Bavinck is not without criticism vis-à-vis the Genevan Reformer, but this criticism does not prevent him from giving expression to his profound admiration for Calvin. It was Calvin, according to Bavinck, whose reforming labors

> completed the Reformation and saved Protestantism. Calvin traced the operation of sin to a wider extent than Luther, to a greater depth than Zwingli. But it is for that reason that the grace of God is more restricted in Luther, less rich in Zwingli, than it is in Calvin. In the powerful mind of the French Re-

former, re-creation is not a system that supplements creation, as in Catholicism, not a religious reformation that leaves creation intact, as in Luther, much less a new creation, as in Anabaptism, but a joyful tiding of the renewal of all creatures. Here the Gospel comes fully into its own, comes to true catholicity. [There is nothing that cannot and ought not to be evangelized.] Not only the church, but also home, school, society and state are placed under the dominion of the principle of Christianity.[26]

With complete conviction, Bavinck chooses Calvin's position and makes it his criterion for judging all kinds of movements and schools that have arisen in the history of the church and theology. Thus, he detects the influence of Roman Catholic dualism in the Socinians and Anabaptists: "The former disregarded the *gratia specialis* and were left with nothing but nature; the latter despised the *gratia communis* and knew of nothing but grace."[27] These two movements exerted a powerful influence also within the churches of the Reformation. The influence of Anabaptism can be shown, for example, in Pietism, the Moravian Church and Methodism."[28] Bavinck does not want to detract in the least from the great achievements of the leaders and pioneers of these movements. Nevertheless, he finds something missing in their Christianity: "The genuine, true catholicity of Christianity is missing." In all these movements

there prevails a restrictive, ascetic view of the world and all its culture. Whether they withdraw themselves into isolation in the Pietist manner, or attack the world in Methodist fashion and attempt to conquer it by main force, never do we find here genuine, true, full reformation; there is only a rescuing and snatching of individuals out of the world, which lies in wickedness; never a methodical, organic reformation of the whole, of the cosmos, of the nation and country. In all these movements, there is an attack on the component parts, not on the center; on the ramparts, not on the fortress itself.

Bavinck characterizes their struggles as "guerilla warfare, weakening the enemy here and there, but not gaining the victory." The world and culture were left to their own devices.[29]

The "glorious truth" of Pietism and related religious movements is that the kingdom of heaven must count as the highest priority. However, the mystical aspect of Christianity must be kept in balance with the ethical, genuinely human aspect:

> Faith appears to be great, indeed, when a person renounces all and shuts himself up in isolation. But even greater, it seems to me, is the faith of the person who, while keeping the kingdom of heaven as a treasure, at the same time brings it out into the world as a leaven.[30]

Liberal theology wanted to restrict Christ's power and word to the heart and the inner chamber, appealing to the fact that his kingdom was not of this world. However, "though it is not *of* this world, it is *in* this world and meant for it."[31] The non-Christian world wants the Christians to withdraw themselves into isolation and to give the world peace and freedom of movement;

> But the catholicity of both Christianity and the church prevents us from complying with this desire. . . . To be sure, the kingdom of God is not of this world, but it does require that everything be subservient to it. It is exclusive, and does not countenance any independent or neutral realm of the world alongside it.[32]

Bavinck is evidently fearful of the danger that a one-sided pietistic attitude would unintentionally abet the secularization of human life advocated by modernism and positivism. For that reason, he does not hesitate to point out the dark side, or rather the fundamental mistake, of this pietism, namely the avoidance of the battle in the social and political arena, and in scholarship.[33] In this Bavinck is opposing, among other things, the introverted attitude, the inclination toward otherworldliness and suspicion of culture, which he observed in the circles of his own *Afgescheiden* Reformed church.[34] He states emphatically that contempt for created life is wrong: "it is in conflict with both Scripture and experience." We must adopt the biblical position, which flatly contradicts this negative evaluation; "Every kind of separatism and asceticism is thereby cut off at the root. All other-worldliness and world-flight is a denial of the first article of the Apostle's creed."[35] When Bavinck discusses the biblical appreciation of created life, he very often refers to 1 Timothy 4:4–5 and 1 John 3:8 ("the Son of God was manifested, not that he might destroy the works of the Father, but that he might destroy the works of the devil, in order thus to restore the works of the Father"). The whole world, then, has been given over to corruption through sin, but through grace it is also being saved in its entirety from sin: "Sin came into the *world*; that is also why God loved the *world*." The word of liberation that comes to us in Christ is therefore not law but gospel: "It is grace alone. And this grace does not abolish nature, but affirms and restores it."[36]

This last phrase expresses the heart of Bavinck's view of the relation of nature and grace. All Bavinck's reflections about this relation can be brought back to this point of departure. This explains the fact that Bavinck brings it up repeatedly in all kinds of formulations. It is the central theme that recurs in number-less variations, the refrain that is unceasingly repeated, the *leit-motif* that we hear everywhere. By way of illustration, we adduce the following quotations (a selection from the many that could be given) that bring this central theme to expression. Bavinck writes,

> So Christianity did not come into the world to condemn and put under the ban everything that existed beforehand and else-where, but quite the opposite, to purify from sin everything that was; and thus to cause it to answer again to its own nature and purpose.[37]

Because revelation is soteriological in content,

> It does not mean an annihilation, but a restoration of God's sin-disrupted work of creation. Revelation is an act of reformation; in re-creation the creation, with all its forms and norms, is re-stored; in the gospel, the law; in grace, justice; in Christ, the cosmos is restored.[38]

Salvation in Christ is "not a second, new creation, but a re-creation." Bavinck continues with these striking words:

> It would have been much simpler if God had destroyed the whole fallen world and replaced it with an entirely new one. But it was his good pleasure to re-establish the fallen world, and to liberate from sin the same mankind that had sinned.[39]

In Roman Catholicism, Christianity may still be *Erlösungsrelig-ion*, but "it is in the first place not *reparatio*, but *elevatio naturae*."[40] However, according to Bavinck's reformational conviction, salvation is precisely *reparatio* of created, natural life. That is why he can maintain the position, over against Roman Catholicism as well as Pietism and Methodism, that nature as God's creation "is in itself of no less value than grace." The Holy Spirit, who acts in continuity with God's directives in natural life, "seeks by his grace to restore the whole of natural life, to liberate it from sin and to hallow it to God."[41] "The kingdom of God is hostile to nothing but sin alone."[42] This insight makes it possible for Bavinck to replace the predominantly ontological and metaphysical Roman Catholic conception with a much more religious and existential approach to the problematics. Consider only the following remarkable statement:

> Grace and sin are opposites; the latter is overcome only by the power of the former; but as soon as the power of sin is broken (and in the same measure that it is) the opposition between God and man disappears.[43]

Grace militates against *sin* in the natural, but it does not militate against the natural itself; on the contrary, it restores the natural and brings it to its normal development, i.e., the development intended by God.[44]

It is therefore a mistake to suppose that grace is restrictive of the capacities and abilities inherent in human nature or renders them inoperative. In an important discussion about revelation and reason, Bavinck argues that there can be no deactivation of reason by revelation: "Grace does not repress nature, including the reason and understanding of man, but rather raises it up and renews it, and stimulates it to concentrated effort."[45]

Special Aspects of Bavinck's View

a) Trinitarian

A number of aspects of Bavinck's conception merit separate attention. In the first place, it should be mentioned that Bavinck puts his basic theme in a *Trinitarian* context. The confession of the Father as Creator "affirms the value of the natural in its own right; the divine origin of all that exists; the original goodness of the world, and within that world of family and society, of scholarship and art, of commerce and industry. There is nothing sinful in itself." "Because sin does not belong to the substance of creation, but is a deformation of that which exists, God can still love the world in spite of the corruption brought about by sin; it still remained his creation, and to that degree good. And he has loved the world "with eternal and almighty love."[46] The love of the Father is evident from the giving of his Son, and the love of the Son is evident from his acceptance of the death of the cross for the sake of the restoration of God's creation:

> The grace of the Son, therefore, extends as far as the love of the Father. It is just as deep in content, just as wide in extent, just as powerful in effect. Nor are any greater limitations put on the regenerating and renewing activity of the Holy Spirit. . . . He grants his indwelling and fellowship to everything the Father has loved and the Son has bought with his blood.[47]

> No other limit is put to the love of the Father, the grace of the Son and the fellowship of the Holy Spirit than that which is established in the ever wise and holy counsel of God. No domain of life is excluded from re-creation. Nothing is in itself beyond redemption or reconciliation. There need be no despair about any of God's creatures.[48]

Within the Trinitarian context, an important place goes to the *Christological* dimension of the theme. Bavinck's Christocentric conception of special revelation, in combination with his conviction concerning the universal soteriological purpose of this revelation, manifests its full significance at this point. The universal range and scope of Christ's deliverance is based on the "soteriological concentration" of Christ's person and work. Jesus, says Bavinck, was not a new legislator, no statesman, no philosopher, etc., but only Jesus, i.e., Savior:

> But *that* he was completely and entirely, not in the narrow sense of Roman Catholics, and Anabaptists and Lutherans, but in the full, deep, broad Reformed sense. Christ did not come only to restore the ethical-religious life of man, and to leave all the rest untouched as though this had not been corrupted by sin and did not stand in need of restoration. No, the love of God, the grace of the Son and the fellowship of the Holy Spirit extend as far as sin.[49]

To be sure, the soteriological concentration of Christ's work may never be lost sight of. Nothing can be compared with the kingdom of God, which he establishes; he who wishes to enter it must deny everything: "the cross is the condemnation of the world and the sentence of death upon all sinful culture." But it is a mistake, Bavinck continues, to deduce from this proclamation "that the gospel is hostile to culture." The gospel of the kingdom may not be isolated from the organic context in which it occurs in history and Scripture. For Christ does not stand at the beginning but makes his appearance in the center of history. He presupposes the work of the Father in creation and providence, including specifically his guidance of Israel. In fact, Christ is the same one who, as the Word, made all things and, in particular, was the life and light of all men. If, therefore, Christ was exclusively proclaimer and founder of the kingdom, Bavinck observes,

> then he cannot have come to destroy the work of the Father, to destroy his own work in creation and providence, but, on the

contrary, to save it from the destruction that man by his sin has inflicted upon it.[50]

In the second place, the proclamation of Jesus may therefore not be isolated either from that which followed it after the crucifixion. The humiliated One is the exalted One:

In his exaltation he takes back what he had denied in his humiliation, but now freed from guilt, cleansed from every spot, regenerated and renewed by the spirit. The resurrection is the restoration in principle of all culture.

For Christ accepted the body in which he had borne the sin of the world on the cross.[51] In the resurrection Bavinck sees his foundational conviction confirmed. He puts it in the following pithy formulation:

The bodily resurrection of Christ from the dead is conclusive proof that Christianity does not adopt a hostile attitude towards anything human or natural, but intends only to deliver creation from all that is sinful, and to sanctify it completely.[52]

It is worthy of note that Bavinck, in this respect, also attaches great weight to the incarnation as such, i.e., irrespective of cross and resurrection. It is instructive what he says about the connection between the denial of Christ's human nature and the contrasting of nature and grace. The denial of the genuine and complete human nature always proceeds, in his view, from a certain dualism, and therefore undermines the confession concerning the Creator and the catholicity of the Christian religion.[53] On the other hand, the unqualified affirmation of Christ's humanity implies, at least in principle, a correct conception of the relation of nature and grace because it makes impossible the devaluation of the earthly and human. The incarnation teaches that the divine *can* reveal itself in a completely human manner.[54] This contains the further implication, of no small importance, that while the human does constitute the organ of sin, the human is not sin itself.

Scripture, writes Bavinck, "maintains, also in the incarnation, the goodness of creation and the divine origin of matter."[55] The incarnation in principle implies "the overcoming of all dualism, the condemnation of ascetism. . . ."[56] Kuitert is right to speak of Bavinck's "anti-spiritualism."[57]

b) Sin/Grace not Substantial

Another important component of Bavinck's conception is his heavy emphasis on the fact that grace *can* restore nature, since sin, no matter how much it may have permeated every sector of created life, is nevertheless "accidental" in the philosophical sense of not belonging to the essence or substance of things. Sin is

> not a substance, but a quality; not *materia*, but *forma*; it is not the essence of things, but rather adheres to the essence; it is a *privatio*, though a *privatio actuosa*, and to that extent contingent, an alien intruder like death. It can therefore be isolated from the essence and removed from it. The world is and remains susceptible to purification and deliverance. Its essence can be saved, and its original state can return.[58]

It is a distinguishing mark of the Christian religion that it maintains the purely ethical nature of sin, and it is enabled to do this by the distinction it makes between creation and Fall. In all systems that identify sin with the substance of things, creation is denatured to a Fall.[59] In Bavinck's judgment, none of the non-Christian religions have succeeded in avoiding this identification of creation and Fall and thus the substantial conception of sin. For him only one religion gives the true perspective on this point, and that is Christianity:[60]

> It is Christianity alone, among all religions, that has conceived of sin as being purely religious and ethical, as being *sin,* has detached it from substance of every kind, and has distinguished it from all physical evil.[61]

Now it is owing to this ethical conception of sin that the view can be maintained that grace restores nature. For in this view

NATURE AND GRACE IN HERMAN BAVINCK

sin, because it is not a substance, could not alter the essence, the substance of creation either. Man as sinner still remains man, and similarly all other creatures, in spite of sin and the reign of corruption, have remained the same in substance and essence. And because sin has not taken away substance, grace does not, as we have seen, give back substance.

> The *materia* of all things is and remains the same, but the *forma*, given in creation, was deformed by sin, to be once again completely reformed by grace.[62]

The non-substantial character of grace is intimately allied to the non-substantial character of sin.

c) Reformation, not Revolution

The next motif to which we draw attention is closely connected with the foregoing. We refer to the fact, frequently and forcefully underscored by Bavinck, *that the reformation that Christ brought about by his revelation differs fundamentally from revolution.* Moses and the prophets, Christ and the apostles "discriminated in an inimitable manner between healthy and sick reality." Whereas in other religions and philosophical systems "these two spheres" are constantly confused and mixed together, the special revelation that comes to us in Christ

> keeps the two in clear distinction; it acknowledges nature, everywhere and without reservation, but it nevertheless joins battle with sin on every front. It seeks the reformation of natural life, always and everywhere, but only for the purpose and by the means of liberating it from unrighteousnss.[63]

This insight is also determinative for the assessment of concrete events and movements in social and political affairs:

> Because the gospel is concerned exclusively with liberation from sin, it leaves all natural institutions intact. It is in principle opposed to all socialism, communism and anarchism, since these never oppose only sin, but identify (through the denial of the Fall) sin with nature, unrighteousness with the very institution of

family and state and society, and thus creation with the Fall. For the same reason the gospel is averse to revolution of any kind, which arises out of the principle of unbelief, since such revolution, in its overthrow of the existing order, makes no distinction between nature and sin, and eradicates the good together with the bad. The gospel, by contrast, always proceeds reformationally. The gospel itself brings about the greatest reformation, because it brings liberation from guilt, renews the heart, and thus in principle restores the right relation of man to God.[64]

What Bavinck calls "the greatest reformation" is the pivot, the dominating center. But out of this center the gospel "makes a reforming and renewing impact on all earthly institutions." The gospel, after all, is a "gospel," "glad tidings for all creatures; not an announcement of destruction and death, but of resurrection and life." The gospel attacks sin alone, but it attacks sin always and everywhere. Now, "by liberating all social conditions and institutions from sin, it also seeks to restore them all according to God's will, and to make them answer to their own nature." As a result, the gospel avoids, on the one hand, the danger of conservatism, which refuses to give attention to change in society, and, on the other hand, revolutionary radicalism, which lacks any constant standpoint in the flux of events.[65] Though averse to every kind of revolution, the Gospel is "all the more concerned for reformation." In its struggle—not against nature as such, but against sin and falsehood—"it proclaims principles that, not through revolutionary, but through moral and spiritual means, have their effect everywhere, which reform and renew everything." It is "a leaven that leavens everything . . .; a principle that recreates everything; a power that overcomes the world."[66]

d) Restoration, not Repristination

A further important point of view is that the redemption by grace of created reality, the reformation of nature, is not merely repristination, *but raises the natural to a higher level than it originally occupied.* In the future, Bavinck writes, the "original order" will be restored. Not, however,

> as though nothing had happened, as though sin had not existed, and the revelation of God's grace in Christ had never occurred. Christ gives more than sin took away; grace did much more abound.[67]

Bavinck is here not indirectly making a case for the notion of an elevation of the natural, as in Roman Catholic theology and elsewhere.[68] We must take into consideration the fact that, according to the conception of Reformed dogmatics (a conception to which Bavinck subscribes), Adam did not yet possess the greatest height: material freedom, the inability any longer to err, to sin, or to die.

> The pre-Fall situation of man, and of the whole earth, was a temporary one, which could not remain as it was. It was of such a nature that it could be raised to a higher glory, but could also, in case of man's transgression, be made subject to vanity and corruption.[69]

Although the latter occurred through sin, grace intends to bring the situation of man and the world to this higher glory. The fact must not be neglected, however, that this higher glory constitutes the goal to which the earth had been directed *from the beginning.* Therefore it is certainly not added to the creation as a *foreign* component. For that reason Bavinck's thesis that reformation through grace is *more* than mere repristination is no denial of his foundational principle that grace restores nature. Bavinck writes that grace

> does not grant anything beyond what Adam, if he had remained standing, would have acquired in the way of obedience. The covenant of grace differs from the covenant of works in the road, not in its final destination. The same benefits are promised in the covenant of works and freely given in the covenant of grace. Grace restores nature and raises it to its highest fulfillment, but it does not add a new, heterogeneous component to it.[70]

In Bavinck's view there is succession and progression, development and ascent in the works of God:

> There is a movement from creation through redemption to sanctification and glorification. The point of arrival returns to the point of departure, and is simultaneously a high point elevated high above the point of departure. The works of God describe a circle that strives upward like a spiral; they are a combination of the horizontal and the vertical line; they move forward and upward at the same time.[71]

It is not necessary, at this point, to explore in greater depth the influence of Bavinck's fundamental theme on the different loci of dogmatic theology.[72] We only point out that the thesis concerning the restoration of nature by grace, in combination with the insight that reformation is more than repristination, is constitutive for Bavinck's eschatology.[73]

Practical Consequences

To complete the overall picture, and to bring it into sharper focus, it remains for us to pay special attention to what Bavinck himself indicated were the *practical consequences* of his fundamental theme, a number of which have already been mentioned in passing in the foregoing discussion. In the first place, we can observe that in this conception the independence of the different societal spheres is fully honored, while at the same time the salutary effect of the gospel in all these spheres is emphatically underscored. Family, society, and state arise out of creation, according to Bavinck, and exist by virtue of *gratia communis*. Bavinck evidently agrees fully with Kuyper's idea of sphere sovereignty. It is also his conviction that sovereignty in these "organic life-spheres" descends directly from God to created reality and that each has a God-given authority of its own.[74] This authority does not in the least imply that the spheres in question have nothing to do with the gospel. On the contrary, they have been corrupted by sin and therefore need the word of God as rule and guide:

> But here again grace does not annul nature. Family, society, and state do experience regeneration by the Spirit of Christ, but they exist and live by virtue of the order of God in nature and retain their full independence alongside the church. Christ did not come to destroy the world and the various spheres of life within it, but to restore and save them.

The same is true of art and scholarship:

> They, like man himself, are conceived and born in sin; but they are not sinful and unclean in themselves. They can be sanctified by the word and the Spirit of Christ. Also for these mighty factors of civilization the gospel is a word of salvation and blessing.[75]

> But here too re-creation is something other than creation. Art and scholarship have their *principium* not in the special grace of regeneration and conversion, but in the natural gifts and talents that God in his common grace grants also to unbelievers.[76]

> The gospel of Christ only serves to liberate art and scholarship from sin and falsehood and to make them answer to their true purpose.[77]

Bavinck thus consciously and intentionally rejects two approaches to the question of the nature-grace relation that have often been taken in the practice of life. On the one hand, he rejects the Roman Catholic attempt to have natural life overarched by a sacral, supernatural superstructure. In this way, grace remains suspended *above* nature. On the other hand, he resists every conception that tends to enclose the gospel within the province of the spiritual life, narrowly conceived, and thus to contrast it with life in the world and human culture. This can happen on the basis of the presuppositions of either an extreme Pietism or a Kantian dualism. The difference between the two, however important in other respects, is irrelevant with respect to the point at issue, insofar as life in the world and human culture is in both cases withdrawn from the effective influence of the gospel. In this way, grace continues to stand *next* to nature. In opposition to this view, Bavinck argues that grace penetrates *into* nature and purifies it from within. For that reason the gospel cannot stand over against nature.

> Sin it condemns, always and everywhere, but marriage and family, society and state, nature and history, art and scholarship, it holds dear. Despite the many failings of those who confess the gospel, it has been through the centuries a rich blessing for all these institutions and activities. The Christian peoples still continue to be the bearers of culture.[78]

To be sure, the gospel is no social or political program, no textbook for science or art; it is the book of God's redemptive revelation, and as such, it has, as we shall see more clearly shortly,[79] a religio-ethical purpose. But precisely in its soteriological concentration, the gospel attains a universal range and scope and has a redemptive impact on the totality of human life. Bavinck willingly subscribes to the view of Calvin, who saw in Christianity

> not merely a principle of new spiritual life, but also an element, the most important element, of culture; to him the Gospel was good news for all creatures, including family, society, scholarship and art.[80]

From this vantage point, we can also understand the vocation of believers in the world. Bavinck's view of this vantage point can perhaps be formulated as follows: the soteriological concentration of Christ's work and word, and the universal range and scope that is based upon it, must be reflected in the lives of believers in such a way that the faith-relation with Christ constitutes not only the decisive pre-condition but also the driving force for the unfolding of created reality in meaningful cultural work. The faith-relation with Christ through the gospel is primary. Man must first become son of God again, before he can become "a cultural creature" in the true sense of the word.[81] But once he *is* son of God, he can also dedicate himself to culture again. With evident agreement he quotes the epigrammatic words of Johann Christoph Blumhardt to the effect "that man must be converted twice, first from the natural to the spiritual life, and thereafter from the spiritual to the natural life."[82] The disciples of Christ do have a calling to bear their cross, to deny themselves, and to follow their Master, but not to practice asceticism and otherworldliness. They must adopt a positive attitude toward earthly life. It is precisely this that was also the intention of the Reformation:

> a Christianity that was hostile, not to nature, but only to sin. . . . In the Reformation the old adage came into its own again: *natura commendat gratiam, gratia emendat naturam.*[83]

Conclusion

Thus, to believers living in fellowship with Christ, the way is opened again to the whole arena of human affairs. All things are theirs, Bavinck writes, inasmuch as and insofar as they are Christ's, and Christ is God's. The reference is to a Pauline text that Bavinck often cites in this context: 1 Corinthians 3:23.[84] Especially in his fine essay on the certainty or assurance of faith, Bavinck has made some beautiful observations about this vocation of believers within the broad horizons of human life. On this point too he is critical of the negative evaluation of social and cultural affairs in the circles of the earlier Pietistic Christians.[85] There can be no doubt that Bavinck is far from poking fun, in the well-known manner (whether with supercilious arrogance or sardonic irony, from the vantage point of a real or imagined cultural superiority), at this Pietistic life style, as at an anachronistic curiosity. He is, rather, of the opinion that this Pietism holds up the mirror to ourselves and opens our eyes to the dangers of an unbridled and unbroken cultural optimism— dangers that Bavinck knew only too well were certainly not imaginary in the circles of his occasionally overzealous fellow-Calvinists. It was his conviction that "this movement [Pietism] gives evidence of an appreciation and concern for the one thing needful, which is only too often absent from us in the busy rush of contemporary life."[86] Against the Pietists, nevertheless, he maintains that the significance of the Christian religion may not be restricted to the redemption and salvation of a few souls.

> The religious life does have its own content and an independent value. It remains the center, the heart, the hearth, out of which all his [i.e., the Christian's] thought and action proceeds and from which it receives inspiration and warmth. There, in fellowship with God, he is strengthened for his labor and girds himself for the battle. But that hidden life of fellowship with God is not the whole of life. The prayer room is the inner chamber, but not the whole dwelling in which he lives and moves. The spiritual life does not exclude domestic and civic, social and political life, the life of art and scholarship. To be sure, it is distinct from these things. It also transcends them by far in value, but it does not constitute an irreconcilable opposition to them; rather, it is the power that enables us faithfully to fulfill our earthly vocation and makes all of life a serving of God.

Here again, Bavinck impresses upon his readers that the kingdom of God is a pearl of great price but, at the same time, a leaven. "Faith is not only the way of salvation, it is also the victory over the world."[87]

> It is in that conviction that the Christian stands and labors—the Christian as he is pictured in the Scriptures, as he makes confession in the Heidelberg Catechism. Being reconciled with God, he is reconciled with all things. Because he confesses the Father of Christ, the Almighty, Creator of heaven and earth, he cannot be narrow in heart or "straitened in his bowels."[88]

> A priest in the Lord's temple, the believer is therefore king of the whole earth. Because he is a Christian, he is a man in the full and truest sense.[89]

In complete agreement with the Reformers, Bavinck holds that we must exercise our Christian faith, in the first place, in the faithful fulfillment of our earthly vocation:

> Roman Catholicism sees the full realization of the Christian
> ideal of life in the monk, in the man who leaves his natural vo-
> cation and devotes himself exclusively to spiritual things.[90]

Moreover, Bavinck notes, "this conception has also had a profound influence in our Protestant circles." To this conception,
according to which a person must do something extraordinary
to be a true Christian and seems to be a Christian "to the same
degree that he ceases to be man," Bavinck takes sharp exception.[91] Also in the practice of the Christian life, we must take
seriously the fact that grace restores the *natural.* Continually and
emphatically, Bavinck insists that the Christian is the true man,
is truly human. As directed to non-Christians, this meant: to be
truly human, in accordance with your Creator's purpose, you
must have faith! As directed to his fellow-Christians, it meant: if
you are a Christian, a Christian in the full sense of the word,
then you are no peculiar, eccentric human being, but you are
fully *human.* To be Christian means to be *human.* It is man's *humanity* that is redeemed. In this connection Bavinck frequently
adduces 2 Timothy 3:17: "that the man of God may be perfect,
thoroughly furnished unto all good works."[92] Bavinck is fully
conscious of the fact that the relation of "human" and "Christian" poses difficult problems, both in theory and practice:

> We continually err on the side of the right or on the side of the
> left. One moment we sacrifice the Christian to the human, and
> the next we sacrifice the human to the Christian. On the one
> side looms the danger of worldliness, on the other side that of
> otherworldliness. Often the Christian life lurches on an un-
> steady path between the two. And yet we hold fast to the con-
> viction that the Christian and the human are not in conflict with
> one another. Often we may not be able to discern intellectually
> the harmony that exists between the two, far less be able to
> demonstrate it in our lives; nevertheless, we believe and we con-
> tinue to believe in the reconciliation and agreement of the two.
> The Christian is the true man, on every front and in every do-

main. Christianity is not opposed to nature, but to sin. Christ came, not to destroy the works of the Father, but only those of the devil.[93]

One day, however, the problems surrounding the relation of human to Christian will find their definitive resolution. This will happen in the *status gloriae,* in which the whole dispensation of grace will have served its purpose and will therefore cease. With this eschatological insight we will deal in the following section.

End Notes

1. Cf. E. P. Heideman, *The Relation of Revelation to Reason in E. Brunner and H. Bavinck* (Assen, 1959), who observes in his analysis of this theme (pp. 191ff.) that Bavinck's idea "that grace does not abolish nature, but renews and restores it . . . may be called the central thought of Bavinck's theology" (p. 196).

2. *De offerande des lofs* (11th impression, Kampen, n.d. [1st ed. 1901]), pp. 44f.

3. *The Philosophy of Revelation* (Grand Rapids, 1953), p. 243 (Dutch: p. 208). For a general indication of the problematics cf. also *De vrouw in de hedendaagsche maatschappij* (Kampen, 1918), p. 28, and "Calvin and common grace," in *Calvin and the Reformation* (London and Edinburgh, 1909), pp. 99f., as well as the fifth thesis of a lecture on creation and re-creation, an extensive report of which appeared in *De Heraut*, no. 1037 (Nov. 7, 1897). This report was reprinted in *De Bazuin* XLV, 47 (Nov. 19, 1897). The theses of this lecture are particularly instructive for the nature/grace theme.

4. *De Bazuin* XLVIII, 12 (March 23, 1900). Cf. also *Offerande des lofs*, p. 45.

5. "De Theologie van Albrecht Ritschl," *Theologische Studiën* VI (1888), 397. Emphasis added. Later, in his *Dogmatics* (IV 703), Bavinck still says that Ritschl's accentuation of the "diesseitige Weltstellung des Menschen" represents an important truth over against the abstract super-naturalism of the Greek and Roman church.

6. For nutshell characterizations of Roman Catholicism and its doctrine see, apart from many passages in the *Dogmatics,* "Calvin and common grace," pp. 104–108; *Het Christendom* (Baarn, 1912), pp. 31–38; and Bavinck's "Algemeene Inleiding" in *Kerkhervorming,* commemorative volume at the fourth centennial, a publication of the Reformed Tract Society "Philippus," 1917, pp. 10–29. In these discussions also Bavinck deals extensively with the Roman Catholic view of the nature/grace relation. To keep the footnotes within reasonable limits we will hereafter refer only occasionally to these passages. Note Bavinck's remarkable characterization of the Roman Catholic system as a "system of complementation": "The Roman Catholic system, at heart Pela-

gian, is one great system of complementation; the image of God complements man, grace complements nature, the evangelical counsels complement the moral precepts. Moreover, this system continues within Christianity: Paul complements Christ, the mass complements his sacrifice, tradition complements the Scriptures, human ordinance complements God's command, love complements faith, the merits of the saints complement the shortcomings of the weak." *De katholiciteit van christendom en kerk* (Kampen, 1888), p. 20 [ET 229–230].

7. *Ibid.*, pp. 9f. [ET 224].

8. *Ibid.*, p. 17 [ET 228].

9. *Ibid.*, p. 18 [ET 228]. Bavinck argues against Harnack, Hatch, and Sohm that not only the gospel but even the Christian church (at least in its first period) was not ascetic. See "Calvin and common grace," pp. 101ff. On asceticism in the early church cf. also IV, 330; *Het christelijk huisgezin* (Kampen, 1908), pp. 67ff.; *Philosophy of Revelation*, pp. 247f. (Dutch, 208f.); *Kennis en leven* (Kampen, 1922) pp. 117ff.

10. *Katholiciteit*, p. 18 [ET 229].

11. *Ibid.*, p. 19 [ET 229].

12. *De algemeene genade* (Kampen, 1894), pp. 20f. [ET 47].

13. *Ibid.*, p. 22 [ET 48].

14. *Ibid.*, 21f. [ET 47f.]. For hierarchy as basic idea cf. *Het Christendom*, p. 38. Bavinck writes in "Calvin and common grace" p. 107: "The whole hierarchical idea is built on the sharp distinction between nature and grace."

15. *De algemeene genade*, p 21. Cf. *Kennis en leven*, p. 135: asceticism is always based on a Pelagian holiness of works.

16. *Katholiciteit*, p. 21[ET 231]. Cf. *Ouders of getuigen* (Kampen, 1901), p. 40 and *Huisgezin*, p. 71: "The Christian element does not permeate the natural, but remains suspended above it; the natural is not renewed but only repressed by it; . . . the leaven is spread out over the dough, but is not kneaded into the bread, so that it is leavened throughout." Cf. also *Bede en rede* (with P. Biesterveld; Kampen, 1898), p. 39 and Bavinck's review of Huizinga's *Herfsttij der Middeleeuwen* [Eng. tr. *The Waning of the Middle Ages*] in *Stemmen des Tijds* IX (1920) 237, in which he says that Huizinga's

book takes us into a world of contrasts: 'The supernatural and the natural stand next to each other in a quantitative, dualistic way, and cannot be reconciled. Each triumphs in turn. The harmony of life is missing; and both Humanism and the Reformation are attempts, each in its own way, to recover it. Cf. *Christelijke wetenschap* (Kampen, 1904), p. 19: in the Middle Ages the natural "was externally repressed, not internally sanctified"; cf. *De algemeene genade*, p.24 [ET 49]. See also note 18. Bavinck's analysis of the doctrine of nature and grace has undoubtedly had a seminal influence on the analysis given in the philosophy of the cosmonomic idea, especially by H. Dooyeweerd. Dooyeweerd distinguishes four religious ground-motives in the development of European philosophic thought: the Greek form/matter motive; the biblical ground-motive of creation, Fall and redemption; the Scholastic ground-motive of nature and grace; and the humanistic ground-motive of nature and freedom. See H. Dooyeweerd, "De vier religieuze grondthema's in den ontwikkelingsgang van het wijsgeerig denken van het avondland," *Philosophia Reformata* VI (1946) 161–179. As a contribution to the structural analysis of the classical Roman Catholic conception, Bavinck's approach retains its significance to this day. Nor is its value diminished, in my view, by the intensive reassessment in later Roman Catholic theology of the questions concerning the relation of nature and grace. On the more recent Roman Catholic discussions, cf. M. C. Smit, *De verhouding van Christendom en historie in de huidige roomskatholieke geschiedbeschouwing* (Kampen, 1950), p. 27ff.; G. C. Berkouwer, "Identiteit of Conflict? Een poging tot analyse," *Philosophia Reformata* XXI (1956) 1–44; Karl Rahner, "Natur und Gnade" in *Fragen der Theologie heute* (herausgegeben von Johannes Feiner, Josef Trütsch und Franz Böckle: Einsiedeln-Zürich-Köln, 1957), pp. 209–230.

17. *De algemeene genade*, p. 23 [ET 48]; I 330 [ET 1.360]; IV 470. On the juxtaposition of the natural and the supernatural order, as this shapes the entire Roman Catholic view of man, cf. *De algemeene genade*, pp. 20ff. [ET 47ff.]. For the characteristically Roman Catholic tendency toward world-flight on the one hand, and toward world domination on the other (both of which arise out of the same dualism), cf. I 330ff. [ET 1.360ff.]; *De algemeene genade*, pp. 23f. [ET 48f]; *Verzamelde Opstellen*, pp. 96f., *Kennis en leven*, pp. 134f. In *Verzamelde Opstellen*, pp. 96f. Bavinck writes: "Both were

born out of a dualism between matter and spirit, which is de-
rived, not from Scripture, but from the philosophy of Plato, and
was transferred within Christianity, in proportion as it became
Roman Catholic, to the distinction of the natural and the supernatural."

18. *Katholiciteit*, p. 28 [ET 235]. On a number of occasions Bavinck
pictures the Reformation as part of the emancipation movement
that came to the fore toward the end of the Middle Ages; cf.
Katholiciteit, pp. 28f. [ET 235f.] *Bede en rede*, pp. 39f.; *Christelijke
Wetenschap*, p. 19, and especially *Verzamelde Opstellen*, p. 97. However, in these and other passages (e.g., *De algemeene genade*, pp.
24f. [ET 49f.]), Bavinck also emphasizes the specifically religious
character of the Reformation, by which it differed fundamentally
from Humanism. Cf. "Algemeene Inleiding" in *De Kerkhervorming*, p. 30: The Reformers "did not contend for the freedom of
the natural, but of the Christian man," cf. *ibid.*, p. 7. Of particular
interest is Bavinck's criticism of the views of Troeltsch on Old
and New Protestantism, and the difference between the two.
The element of truth in this lies in the recognition of the fundamental difference between Reformation and Revolution. For the
Reformation, in contrast with the Enlightenment, continued to
move within the bounds of historic Christianity; it had no other
concern than to restore this Christianity in its purity. Materially,
the Reformation is closer to Roman Catholicism than to the
Revolution. But Bavinck objects to the view that the Reformation in fact remained medieval. This is to fall into two miscon-
ceptions, in his view. The first is the identification of the
supernaturalism of medieval Catholicism with the supernatural
character that has distinguished Christianity from the beginning.
The Reformation retained the latter, but brought about a fundamental and radical change in the medieval conception of the
relation between supernatural revelation and nature. The second
misconception consists in the failure to do justice, in this approach, to the originality and the significance of the Reformation (*ibid.*, pp. 6ff., cf. also *Philosophy of Revelation*, pp. 3ff. [Dutch,
pp. 2ff.]. This originality of the Reformation emerges especially
in the fact that it replaced the quantitative opposition of the
natural and the supernatural with the qualitative one of sin and
grace; cf. I 331 [ET 1.361], IV 390f., *Ouders of getuigen*, 49f.

19. "Calvin and common grace," p. 127. On the significance of the Reformation for ethics, cf. *De ethiek van Ulrich Zwingli* (Kampen 1880), pp. 3ff.

20. *De algemeene genade*, p. 44 [ET 60].

21. *Katholiciteit*, p. 29 [ET 236]. Cf. *Johannes Calvijn* (Kampen, 1909), pp. 33f. and *Bijbelsche en religieuze psychologie* (Kampen, 1920), p. 90: the Reformation in principle overcame the dualism of spirit and matter. On the healthy piety of the Reformers, cf. *Katholiciteit*, pp. 29f. [ET 237f.] and *De zekerheid des geloofs* (Kampen, 1901), pp. 42f. [ET 38f.].

22. *Katholiciteit*, p. 30 [ET 236].

23. III 581 [ET 3.577].

24. III 582 [ET 3.577, where "another grace" should read "no other grace"].

25. III 583f. [3.578f.]. On the Roman Catholic concept of grace in its opposition to that of the Reformation, cf. II 499ff. [ET 2.537ff.], III 513 [ET 3.517], IV 423, 473ff., and especially *Roeping en Wedergeboorte* (Kampen, 1903), pp. 195ff.

26. *Katholiciteit*, p. 32 [ET 237f]. Cf. also above Chapter I, section 3.3 and the present chapter 2, section 2a, note 40. One of Bavinck's criticisms of Calvin concerns the latter's conception of the relation between church and state, cf. e.g., *Johannes Calvijn*, p. 24. On Bavinck's preference for Calvin above Luther and Zwingli, cf. also, besides the passage referred to in my article "Calvijn en Bavinck," *Opbouw* III, 15 (July 10, 1959); IV 390ff.; *Our Reasonable Faith* (Grand Rapids, 1956), pp. 125f. (Dutch: *Magnalia Dei* [Kampen, 1931], pp. 111f.), "Calvin and Common Grace," pp. 11ff., 123 and especially Bavinck's speech on September 22, 1892 at the Fifth General Council of the Alliance of the Reformed Churches holding the Presbyterian System, held in Toronto, September 21–30, 1892. See the *Proceedings* of this Council (London, 1892), pp. 48–55, especially pp. 49ff.; cf. the account of this speech in V. Hepp, *Dr. Herman Bavinck* (Amsterdam, 1921), pp. 215ff. Bavinck's view of Luther is criticized by G. T. Rothuizen, *Primus usus legis; studie over het burgerlijk gebruik van de wet* (Kampen, 1962), pp. 47f., and W. Krusche, *Das Wirken des Heiligen Geistes nach Calvin* (Berlin, 1957), p. 98.

27. *De algemeene genade*, pp. 30ff. [ET 53ff.]. Cf. I 158f. [ET 1.183f.], *Our Reasonable Faith*, p. 126 (Dutch: p. 112), and *Het Christendom*, pp. 49ff. On Anabaptism, cf. the places listed in the *Register* of IV and furthermore especially *Roeping en Wedergeboorte*, pp. 98ff., 145, 148f. Like Roman Catholicism, Anabaptism is based on the opposition of nature and grace: "The difference is that Anabaptism makes that opposition absolute and thus annihilates nature; Roman Catholicism "views the opposition as a relative one, and suppresses nature," IV 396, cf. 415: Roman Catholicism does not look upon the natural as sinful, as Anabaptism does, but teaches that the natural is of a lower order; for this view of Roman Catholicism cf. also *Verzamelde Opstellen*, p. 97. For a comparison of Calvinism, Lutheranism, and Anabaptism, see *Alliance Proceedings*, pp. 52f.

28. *De algemeene genade*, p. 33 [ET 54]. For the various movements mentioned in the text, cf. the passages listed in the *Register* of IV. On Pietism cf. also *Zekerheid des geloofs*, pp. 39ff. [ET 41ff.]; (see what follows in the text) and section 3, 2ff. below; on the previously mentioned Moravians, discussed together with the Methodists, cf. *Zekerheid des geloofs*, pp. 49ff. [ET 45ff.]. On Methodism, cf. also *Roeping en Wedergeboorte*, pp. 172ff.; on asceticism in Roman Catholicism, Anabaptism, Pietism and Methodism, cf. *Paedagogische Beginselen* (Kampen, 1904), pp. 31f., cf. *Bijbelsche en religieuze psychologie*, p. 147. Bavinck writes in IV 417: "Avoidance is the word of the Anabaptists; asceticism that of the Roman Catholics; renewal and sanctification that of the Protestant, particularly of the Reformed Christian."

29. *Katholiciteit*, pp. 44f. [ET 246f.]; cf. the corresponding passage in III 571.

30. *Katholiciteit*, pp. 47f. [ET 248f.].

31. *De algemeene genade*, p. 47 ET 62].

32. *Katholiciteit*, pp. 48f. [ET 248f.].

33. Cf. *Katholiciteit*, p. 49 [ET 249].

34. Cf. what Bavinck writes about the oration *Katholiciteit* to his friend Snouck Hurgronje, as quoted in V. Hepp, *Dr. Herman Bavinck*, p. 147: "No doubt you have received my oration. Bear in mind as you read it that it is especially meant as a kind of antidote to the separatistic and sectarian tendencies that sometimes manifest

themselves in our church. There is so much narrow-mindedness, so much parochialism among us, and the worst of it is that this counts for piety." J. H. Gunning II, *Het protestansche Nederland*, 65, n.1, made the following comment about *Katholiciteit* : "One hardly believe his eyes if he reads Dr. Bavinck's rectorial oration *The Catholicity of Christianity and the Church* (1888) and bears in mind that this beautiful, truly broad conception of Theology and Scholarship is being entertained and defended in the auditorium of the Kampen Theological Seminary. What will be the result in ecclesiastical practice if Dr. Bavinck's students attempt to bring into effect these splendid principles of their teacher?" We would like to draw attention also, at this point, to the important judgment on *Katholiciteit* made by H. Berkhof in his work *De Katholiciteit der Kerk* (Nijkerk, 1962), pp. 20f. After pointing out that the rise to dominance of the doctrine of the invisible church in the nineteenth century had led to a waning of interest in the visible church, and consequently also in its catholicity, Berkhof writes that *Katholiciteit*, to his knowledge, is the "only important exception" to this rule. "We find in it a genuine renewal of the idea of catholicity. The oration is distinctive, on the one hand, by its liberality and breadth, and on the other, by its modernity." It is noteworthy (to make a parenthetical observation) that Berkhof fails to mention Gunning in this connection. Berkhof is correct in making the observation that Bavinck in his oration uses the word "catholicity" in a double sense—in the first place in the meaning of the contemporary word "ecumenicity," and in the second place in the markedly qualitative meaning of "sanctification of the whole of earthly reality." But a qualification must be made when Berkhof goes on to say that Bavinck's oration has an isolated position even within his own literary output. It is true enough of catholicity in the first sense (Bavinck indeed has only isolated statements on the "ecumenicity" of the church), but it is not true (as this whole section demonstrates) of catholicity in the broader, qualitative sense. It is clear, however, that the use of the concept in this sense is concerned less with the catholicity of the church than with the catholicity of revelation, or of Christianity and faith.

35. *De algemeene genade*, p. 45 [ET 60].

36. *Ibid.*, p 48 [ET 62]. This saying is also repeatedly quoted by Bavinck in the Latin form of the famous Thomistic thesis: *Gratia non tollit*

naturam, sed perficit. On this thesis, as it functions in Roman Catholic theology, cf. O. Weber, *Grundlagen der Dogmatik* (Neukirchen, 1955–62), I 693 and II 582, who also indicates the possibility of using the thesis in another sense, *ibid.* I 471 and 639, n. 1. When Bavinck renders *perficit* as "restores," it is plain that this involves a certain modification of the original meaning; cf. F. H. von Meyenfeldt, "Prof. Dr. Herman Bavinck: 1854–1954 'Christus en cultuur'," *Polemios* I, 21 (Oct. 15, 1954), p. 110, n. 11.

37. "Inleiding," in *Christendom en opvoeding* (Baarn, 1908), p. 9. It should be noted that Bavinck (as is evident from the foregoing) often uses the concepts Christianity," "religion," etc. as equivalents of "revelation."

38. *Christelijke wereldbeschouwing* (Kampen, 1913), p. 89; cf. IV, 358. On the law-gospel relation in this connection, cf. the following section.

39. IV 675f.

40. II 508 [ET 2.547].

41. III 575 [ET 3.571].

42. *Our Reasonable Faith*, p. 528 (Dutch: p. 507).

43. III 577 [ET 3.573].

44. Cf. *Offerande des lofs*, pp. 43f. and *Het christelijk huisgezin*, pp. 57ff.

45. *De Bazuin* XLIX, 43 (October 25, 1901). This article, entitled "Openbaring en rede" is actually a review of a publication by A. Anema, but in fact Bavinck takes this as an occasion to set forth his own views. Heideman did not make use of this article. But its import (see the text) is in complete accord with his findings. In addition, cf. I 588 [ET 1.618]: revelation does not conflict with human reason *per se*, but only *per accidens corruptionis et pravae dispositionis*.

46. *Bede en rede*, p. 34. Cf. *Philosophy of Revelation*, p. 107 (Dutch: p. 91): "The doctrine of creation maintains the divinity, the goodness and sacredness of all created things." The recognition of creation opens the possibility for man of a "free and royal relation" to nature, devoid of both the deification and the contempt of nature" (*ibid.* 105f.; Dutch: 89ff.). On the love of God, cf. section "g" below.

47. *Bede en rede*, pp. 35f.

48. *Ibid.*, p. 40.

49. *De algemeene genade*, p. 47 [ET 61].

50. *Philosophy of Revelation*, p. 267 (Dutch: p. 229). On Christ's appreciation of natural life, which he saves through his work of redemption, cf. *Offerande des lofs*, pp. 49ff.; *Philosophy of Revelation*, pp. 255ff. (Dutch: pp. 219ff.); *Verzamelde Opstellen*, pp. 133ff.

51. *Philosophy of Revelation*, p. 267 (Dutch: p. 230).

52. *Offerande des lofs*, p. 52. cf. *Katholiciteit*, p. 10 [ET 223]: "Christianity is the religion of the cross. The mystery of suffering is its center. . . . Nevertheless, the reverse side is not missing. The cross may cast a shadow over all of nature, but the resurrection shines its light also over it." Cf. "Calvin and common grace," p. 101.

53. III 280f. [ET 3.297f.].

54. *Kennis en leven*, p. 39.

55. *Our Reasonable Faith*, p. 325 (Dutch: p. 307).

56. *De vrouw in de hedendaagsche maatschappij*, p. 27. In rejecting dualism, Bavinck elsewhere mentions creation, incarnation and resurrection in one breath. In *Bijbelsche en religieuze psychologie*, pp. 57f., he writes: "Creation, incarnation and resurrection are conclusive proofs that spirit and matter, however they may differ, are susceptible to union and cooperation." Cf. also *ibid.*, p. 90. As we noted above, under section "a," Bavinck was of the opinion that the possibility of the incarnation was given with creation. H. M. Kuitert, *De mensvormigheid Gods* (Kampen, 1962), p. 116, n. 113, puts it well: for Bavinck "the whole creation is a paradigmatic combination-possibility between matter and spirit, and for that reason the possibility-ground for the incarnation."

57. *Ibid.*, p. 127. Bavinck's high view of the body is striking, cf. II 521 [ET 2.559]: "The body is no prison, but a wonderful art-piece of God almighty, which constitutes the nature of man as much as the soul does." Bavinck even says that it is "characteristically Reformed not to neglect the body," *De Jongelingsvereeniging in hare beteekenis voor het sociale leven* (1917), p. 4. On the rejection of asceticism and dualism in connection with the family, cf. *Huisgezin*, pp. 113f. Bavinck here (*ibid.*, pp. 114f.) also draws attention to the naturalness with which the Scriptures speak about

sexuality. They adopt the standpoint of a "healthy realism," although on the other hand they also avoid all libertinism.

58. *De algemeene genade*, pp. 45f. [ET 60f.].

59. *Philosophy of Revelation*, p. 231, cf. 306f. (Dutch: p. 197, cf. 265).

60. *Ibid.*, p 265 (Dutch: pp. 306).

61. *Christelijk wereldbeschouwing*, p. 86; cf. *Bijbelsche en religieuze psychologie*, p. 90.

62. II 535 [ET 2.574]. Cf. *Verzamelde Opstellen*, p. 107: Christianity conceived of the disharmony in the world "as a temporal, occasional *deformitas*, and explained it, not in terms of the nature of things, of *materia*, but in terms of the anomaly, the *anomia* of things; i.e., not physically, but ethically." For the non-substantial character of grace Bavinck's comments on regeneration at IV 69 are instructive. Among other things, he says there, Christ is "not a second Creator," but "Reformer of all things." A good analysis of Bavinck's concept of substance was given by J. M. Spier in a long series of articles on the concept of substance in the paper *Pro Ecclesia* VI–VII (1940–1942). Articles XIX–XXV and XXIX deal with Bavinck.

63. *Huisgezin*, pp. 82f., cf. "Calvin and common grace," p. 128.

64. *Verzamelde Opstellen*, p. 149. Cf. II 538 [ET 2.578].

65. *Verzamelde Opstellen*, pp. 149f. Bavinck identified his position with the names of the two Protestant political parties existing at that time in the Netherlands, namely the Christian-Historical Union and the Anti-Revolutionary Party. "Christian" refers to the constant standpoint, and "historical" to change, whereas "anti-revolutionary" gives the additional qualification that the Christian-historical principles must be practically applied, not by means of a radical revolution but by a reformation that retains the good (*ibid.*, p. 150). For an eloquent defense of reformation as opposed to repristination, cf. *Christelijke en neutrale staatkunde* (Hilversum, 1905), p. 30.

66. IV 376.

67. *De algemeene genade*, p. 43 [ET 59]. According to Bavinck, the Reformed theologians had a better insight into this than the Lutherans; cf. the characterization of both standpoints in II 533ff. [ET 2.572ff.] and III 582 [ET 3.577]. Cf. the objections of W.

Trillhaas, *Dogmatik* (Berlin, 1962), p. 248, against the "Restitu-tionschristologie," which he finds, in a specific form, "im neuen Luthertum, besonders in dessen bürgerlichen Ausprägung etwa durch die Ritschlsche Theologie."

68. Cf. Berkouwer's comments on the notion of "elevatio," partially in connection with H. Berkhof's objections against the exclusive defense of the traditional "restoration" theme (*De wederkomst van Christus* II [Kampen, 1963], pp. 267ff.).

69. III 163 [3.182].

70. III 582 [3.577].

71. *Our Reasonable Faith*, p. 144 (Dutch: pp. 128f.); cf. I 347f. [1.376f.] and II 400 [2.436].

72. The impact of the basic theme on the doctrine of the covenant was noted above, under section 2.

73. Cf. IV 698ff. Bavinck's entire eschatology could be considered an elaboration of what he says in *De algemeene genade*, p. 46, about the Christian religion: "It does not make a new cosmos, but makes the cosmos new."

74. *Ibid.*, pp. 50f. The church does not stand above these life-spheres, as Roman Catholicism teaches, but *next* to them. Domination over the church by the state, or domination over the state by the church are therefore both illegitimate (*ibid.*). S. P. van der Walt, *Die wijsbegeerte van Dr. Herman Bavinck* (Potchefstroom, 1953), p. 136, n. 18 mistakenly claims that Bavinck never uses the term "sphere-sovereignty," although he advocates the conception it-self. Bavinck not only advocates the conception, but on a num-ber of occasions also uses the term; cf. *Kennis en leven*, pp. 48, 201: *De Bazuin* L, 15 (Apr. 11, 1902).

75. *De algemeene genade*, p. 51 [ET 64]. Cf. *Philosophy of Revelation*, p. 258 (Dutch: p. 222): the Gospel is not opposed to culture, but is "the most important element of all culture,—principle and goal of what all culture in the genuine sense of the word strives after, and must strive after."

76. *De algemeene genade*, p. 52 [ET 64]. Cf. above section "2d."

77. On scholarship cf. *Bede en Rede*, p. 37 and *Christelijke wetenschap*, p. 121.

78. *Philosophy of Revelation*, p. 269 (Dutch: p. 231).

79. Cf. below section 3, 1 (j) aa.

80. *Evangelisatie* (Utrecht, 1913), p. 30.

81. *Philosophy of Revelation*, p. 266 (Dutch: p. 229).

82. *Ibid.*, p. 242 (Dutch: p. 207).

83. I 332 [ET 1.362].

84. *Offerande des lofs*, p. 53.

85. *Zekerheid des geloofs*, p. 99 [ET 93].

86. *Ibid.*, p. 100 [ET 94].

87. *Ibid.*, p 101f. [ET 95f.].

88. *Ibid.*, p. 102. For this idea see section "2d" above. On the combination of faith and science, cf. e.g., *Paedagogische beginselen*, p. 52, and on faith and politics *Christelijke en neutrale staatkunde*, pp. 39f.

89. *Zekerheid des geloofs*, p. 103 [ET 96f.].

90. On the Reformation's revaluation of one's earthly vocation, cf. *Paedagogische beginselen*, p. 96, "Calvin and common grace," p. 123. Cf. also IV 703f.

91. *De algemeene genade*, pp 48f. [ET 62f.].

92. Cf. e.g., *Christelijke wetenschap*, pp. 107f. and *Paedagogische beginselen*, pp. 30ff. ("the beautiful text") and 49ff. (a very important passage for our theme). For criticism of Bavinck's use of this text, see S. O. Los, *Moderne paedagogen en richtingen* (Amsterdam, 1933), pp. 173f. On the relationship of the *christianum* to the *humanum*, Bavinck's words in *Paedagogigche beginselen*, p. 50, are of interest: "Christianity and humanity are one." In this context, Bavinck evidently means by these words that Christianity is the true humanity, not vice versa. Whether he accepts or rejects the converse (i.e., the idea that true humanity is *ipso facto* Christian) cannot be determined with complete certainty. For on the one hand, Bavinck says (*Hedendaagsche moraal* [Kampen, 1902], p. 51), "Humanity without divinity turns into bestiality." Yet on the other hand, he writes (*De welsprekendheid* [Kampen, 1889], p. 64), "Whatsoever things are true, or good, or lovely among our opponents, whatsoever things are of good report, in whatever area, in the domain of art and science, that is Christian."

93. *De Bazuin* L, 41 (Sept. 26, 1902). On the theme of human and Christian, cf. already *De ethiek van Ulrich Zwingli*, p. 1.

GLOSSARY OF LATIN AND OTHER FOREIGN TERMS

page

10, 14   *donum superadditum* – "gift added on"

10   *visio Dei* – "vision of God"

12   *foedus gratiae* – "covenant of grace"

13   *ut elevet et sanet* – "to elevate and heal"

13   *per accidens* – "by 'accident'" [cf. p. 22], i.e., "incidentally," "non-essentially"

13   *ex condigno* – "by merit"

14, 22, 23   *forma* – "form"

15   *gratia specialis* – "special grace"

15, 27   *gratia communis* – "common grace"

17   *Afgescheiden* (Dutch) – "Secessionist," i.e., belonging to the 1834 Secession or *Afscheiding* from the Dutch Established Church.

17   *leitmotif* (German) – "dominant recurring theme"

18   *Erlösungsreligion* (German) – "religion of redemption

18   *reparatio* – "restoration"

18   *elevatio naturae* – "elevation of nature"

22   *privatio* – "lack," "absence"

22   *privatio actuosa* – "active lack"

27   *principium* – "principle"

29   *natura commendat gratiam, gratia emendat naturam* – "nature commends grace, grace emends nature"

32   *status gloriae* – "state of glory"

note

5   *diesseitige Weltstellung des Menschen* (German) – "the position of man in this [earthly] world"

36   *gratia non tollit naturam, sed perficit* – "grace does not abolish nature, but perfects it."

45   *per accidens corruptionis et pravae dispositionis* – "by the 'accident' [cf. p. 11] of corruption and evil disposition"

62   *deformitas* – "deformity," "misshapenness"

62   *anomia* (Greek) – "lawlessness"

67   *im neuen Luthertum, besonders in dessen bürgerlichen Ausprägung etwa durch die Ritschlsche Theologie* (German) – "in modern Lutheranism, especially in its bourgeois expression, for example in the theology of Ritschl."

92   *ipso facto* – "by the very fact"

Printed in the United States
135109LV00004B/6/A